Homesick

Faraway

Life is a process of repeatedly
finding things that leave until we
eventually find the things that stay.

It is beautiful; then it is tragic.
It is beautiful; then it is tragic.

This goes on and on until it
is only beauty that remains.

Chapters:

Chapter One:

And Then I Met You

I've always adored the look in your eyes;
there's always been something so damn
beautifully tragic about them. One look
at you, and anyone could tell that you've
been places, dark places, places you still
often think about but never speak about -
not to a single soul for a single reason.

I'd count the seconds until you'd look away,
until someone or something else had caught
your eye. It was in those few seconds wherein
I could get lost in them without you knowing,
without giving it away that I was lost at sea,
capsized and captivated, waxing and waning
above and under the water that was the lovely
lostness in those eyes of yours.

I'd see them every time my eyes closed at night.
And every time I'd blink, I'd hold them shut for
just a second longer, if only to feel the feeling of
being looked at by you for one-sixtieth of a single
moment longer.

And one night, one brilliant, unusually-luminous
autumn evening, my eyes lined up in your line of
sight, just right for you to be able to see something
in my headlights as well. The dark voids inside of
us leapt from our bodies, lifted toward the stars.

And in that moment, everything that was ever
wrong with us and our lives seemed to float off,
as if they finally decided to leave us alone, as if
they knew they stood no chance against the sheer
happiness that was about to come into our lives.

Your life was miserable, and then you met me.
My life was unbearable, **and then I met you.**

1

I was lost in this world,
wandering blindly with
a heart so broken I could
see no point in even trying
to put it back together.

But then I found you,
and that no longer seemed
to make any sense to me.

And in the process of falling
madly, wildly, incomparably
hard for you, I found a reason
to take those pieces and put them
all back where they belonged.

   - I wanted my heart again.
   I needed you to feel it.

I saw you, and
I knew right away
that I wanted you
in my life forever.

- *the moment we met*

Hope is what leads
to disappointment, yet
I still cant stop hoping
for a life of happiness
together with you.

And that shocks me,
because minutes before
we had met, I was entirely
convinced that I would
never hope in anything
ever again.

I am in love with you,
and I have no say in it.

It happens, it happens,
and it keeps on happening.

And I sometimes find
myself wondering if maybe,
just maybe, I had a little bit
of control over this,
would I still stay here?

Would I knowingly choose
these lingering, never-ending
explosions in my chest, or
would I choose the silence
of never having loved?

Every time, I choose
the explosions, the violent
displays of heaven having
once lived in my chest.

I choose to feel.
I choose to be alive.

- heaven in my heart

The story of us
began at birth:
I entered this world
and immediately began
my search for you.

I'd change who I am
to keep things between
us from changing.

I'd surrender my self
to keep us how we are –
take a chisel to my soul
to sculpt someone better.

You are my only necessity
in a world stuffed with things
I could honestly do without.

Even when our hearts have
different postal codes, our souls
are still together all the same.

  - *with us, it makes no difference.*
    we are always together.

Our love is rare:
it's innocent, honest,
thoughtful - like the way
we wipe each other's tears
when saying goodbye.

You're the only thing
that chokes me up: after
years of feeling nothing,
you've gifted me the ability
to shed tears again.

I don't know what our future looks like.
I could not tell you. All I know is that with
each and every day, we slowly creep, just
one more footstep, into that dimly lit thing
we call the rest of our lives together. It is
beautiful. It is daunting. It both fills my
heart with happiness and terrifies me to
my very core in equal parts. And most days,
I find myself standing outside, looking for
any trace of a shooting star to wish upon
that everything works out, that, in the end,
we get everything we have ever wanted.

- tomorrow and how I see it tonight

In all honesty,
we're just two broken
humans who make each
other feel undeniably
whole again.

I shut my eyes and think of you,
and suddenly I am somewhere else.
There is no bedroom around me.
I don't feel these sheets, the pillows.
I sense no time nor temperature.
All that bothered me wanders off.
The overcast outside leaves.

This is the escape I have for now;
I don't belong being away from you.

 - *I never liked this bedroom, anyway.*

When I miss you too much,
I touch something you've touched.
It brings you right here back to me,
and everything is all okay again.

- *sweaters with you on them*

Beautiful is the way
love inspires you to
want to be better.
You stay up late after
they've fallen asleep
just to make plans.
You look at how you've
been living and think of
ways to do it better.
You consider them,
and you change to make
your soul more gorgeous.
And you don't do this
just for them; no, they'll
have you as you are.
You do it because
you want it.

That night,
I kissed your lips
and a weight was lifted.
We were together,
and we were home.

 - *love in an airport*

You did the
seemingly impossible,
gifted me buoyancy in
the very same waters
that used to drown me.

You would lay next to me
when I felt as if I were sinking,
and you would tell me the truth:
*"this is all in your head;
everything will be okay."*

  - my guardian angel

True love is a lot like
two people grabbing ahold
of each other by their souls
and refusing to let the other
one go, to let the other one
ever be truly unhappy.

- what we have

The right one
will love you the
hardest when you
need it the most.

Soulmates always
find their way back
to each other.

You'll know it on sight.
You'll feel it deep down
inside of you that no matter
how much time passes,
nothing will change the
way you feel – nothing
will make the love
go away.

Every time we see each other,
you leave landmarks in my head,
little vacation spots for me to visit
whenever I'm feeling alone.

- happy memories

I'm so drunk on our feelings,
if you ever left, I'd probably be
hung-over for the rest of my life.

And I know that they say obsession
is for the insecure, but I don't mind
people thinking that of me if it means
I get to feel this alive forever.

Chapter Two:

Homesick

You call again and say,
"I still have hope for us."

It's right then when it hits,
the sudden lightning strike
that is the pity and sadness
I feel for myself.

I shouldn't have answered,
but I always do it for you.
I always cave in and let you
break my heart a little bit
more all over again.

You come over, and you
get sick of me, so you leave.
Then I sit alone and get sick
of feeling like I'm an idiot.

I do my best to move on,
but the small steps forward
I take when you're away
are nothing compared to the
giant leaps backward I take
every time I let you back in.

Someday, I'll shut the door.
Someday, I'll lock you out and
turn this dimly lit household
into a happy home once again.

Before I met you,
I never considered myself
poetic, but there's an odd
poetry in wanting what
we cannot have.

I miss hearing raindrops on my car in the background
as we sat there and learned about each other through
the night. I miss the butterflies of a first kiss. I miss the
way the world vanished when we spoke to each other.
I miss so many things, the little ones, the mundane
ones, the life changing ones - all of the things that
I could never get back.

We used to feel so connected,
but, these days, I've lost all sight
of the bridges that used to connect us.

They say healing takes time,
that time heals all wounds,
so I wait, I wait, and I wait.

And while every clock I see
ticks ahead like I know them to,
time has stalled in my head.

I am still right back there,
right in your arms with every-
thing feeling right in the world.

So tell me, what good is time if
nothing ever changes in me?

I'm beginning to think that time
heals nothing, but that we can
eventually heal ourselves if we
are given enough time.

You disappeared just as quickly
as you came, and I didn't even ask
you why, because knowing why and
where you went doesn't make it hurt
any less; if anything, it just makes me
wonder more what the hell is so very
wrong with me that people can be in
love with me one day and out of it
the next.

I know I shouldn't, but I wish we
could talk still. I wouldn't really know
what to say to you if I could. It's so
confusing, being in love with somebody
you know you shouldn't be in love with.
You let go so long ago, but my fingers
are still breaking and healing from
repeatedly holding onto and letting
go of hope. I need to pick which side
of the fence I need to fall onto. I will
never truly heal if I don't, and, believe
me, I want to heal – I truly do. It's
just hard to make a decision when
both sides of the fence are equally
as beautiful.

Some nights,
I still find it hard
not to call you.

We haven't
talked in ages,
yet my feelings
haven't aged
a day.

You're always in the middle:
far away enough from love to feel safe,
but close enough to it to make me believe
that you just might feel it someday.

Maybe, it wasn't love.
Maybe, we just made each
other feel less miserable,
and maybe that was all
we truly needed then –
maybe, that was why it
always felt so right.

I saw it coming, like dark clouds looming off
in the distance - the eventual last time I'd feel our
fingers interlock, the final time our body heat would
keep each other warm at night, the pain of someday
knowing you're over me enough to move on and start
looking for love and comfort in other people. I knew
this day would come; I knew my soul would split
in half, but being aware that pain is coming
doesn't make the shock of it hurt any less.

I'm longing for you.
It's making my bones hurt.
My soul shivers from the
cold of you not being here.

I feel so miserable, and
there's not a single thing
I can think to do to make
myself feel better tonight.

I need you; I just need you,
and that scares me because
I've never needed anyone
or anything else before.

I want to pick up my phone
and tell you how stupid it is
that we don't talk anymore,
all about how soulmates are
supposed to be together.

But I already know where
that road leads, and my feet
are already blistered from
walking miles and miles
with the weight of this
relationship on my back.

Knowing this, still,
I'm longing for you,
and my soul wont stop
its endless shivering.

Year by year, brick by
brick, disappointment after
disappointment, I gradually
built up walls around my heart –
a watchtower for every corner –
to keep the world out, to
disallow other people the
chance to ruin me again.

And for a while now, I have
lived by this mantra, carved
it in stone on the inside of
every inch of every wall
and watchtower:

"I am alone, but I am safe."

- tucked in and healing

I always knew that someday
we'd have to say goodbye; I guess,
I just tucked that truth away and
chose to believe that maybe if I
didn't look at the monster, it
wouldn't sink its claws into me.

  - *even my bones wish you were here*

It's not going to
sleep that's hard;
it's falling back to
sleep after I have
dreamt of you again
that keeps me up.

- goodnight again

And every morning,
I deal with the fact
that you fell asleep
with someone else
last night.

- *my days die at daylight*

People tell me to move on,
but what they don't understand
is that when I promised you this
forever of mine, I meant it with
all that I have in me.

I lie quietly in my bed,
and suddenly I'm besieged,
abruptly overtaken, by the
feeling that something in
my life is not right.

When things are going well,
I unsettle myself; I tear the
apartments in my mind apart
searching for something
to feel uneasy about.

Because,
life has taught me that if
you are happy where you are,
you have stopped running,
and that leaves time for
karma to catch up with you.

I should want
to be around you.

I shouldn't
want to go on these
drives to nowhere.

They're just excuses
to tell you "I'm busy."

I should return your calls.
I should kiss you in public.
I should let you close to me.

And
I'm sorry for not
treating you better,
but, believe me,
someday,

someone else will.

My days are spent
tiptoeing on a fence
between feeling too much
and feeling nothing at all.

I never meant
to break your heart.

If only millions of
apologies could heal
the millions of cracks

I've left behind.

Some days,
it feels as if I am
standing with glass
walls all around me.

The wall behind me
keeps me from touching
all that I have touched.

The wall in front of me
keeps me from touching
all that I could touch.

The walls beside me
keep me from feeling
anything around me.

The wall above me is
there just to keep me
from escaping.

   *- I'm in love, but I
   can't feel your skin*

I hope you think of me on the
coldest nights, when warm bodies
and new affections only leave you
frozen and empty. And I hope it
hits you like a ton of bricks: I'm
the standard on which you gauge
everyone else: I'm that one heart
you wish you never touched
and left broken.

My ghosts don't look like
everyone I've loved and lost;
they look like everyone I love
that I'll lose someday if I can't stop
being this person I've become.

I fall asleep
not because I
need sleep, but
because I hope
that things will
be different when
I wake up.

When you disappeared the way
you did, you reserved no right to
reappear: the night you left, you
lost your place in my life.

I am unhappy, but I
don't want to be anymore.
I cling to this, the fact that,
in my darkest hour, I still
have faith in myself, hope
that things will someday
turn around for me.

Chapter Three:

It's Okay to Feel

I've lost so much love;
I've lost so many feelings
and the ability to feel alive.

I've lost temporary people;
I've lost the things I thought
would never see an end.

I've lost my mind.
I've lost sight of what truly
matters in my life in the end.

I've lost my heart; I'd put
my hand over my chest just
to check if it's still there.

I've lost time.
I've lost my way.
I've lost nearly everything
there is to lose in this life.

And of all the things I've lost,
the most important one I am
getting back is the idea that
it's okay to feel.

It's okay to try again.
It's okay to put myself out there.
It's okay if I give something my
everything, just for it to fall
apart in the end.

This is the way of life;
we lose things, so many things,
until we find the ones that stay.

- it's okay to feel

Losing you
forced me to
rethink everything.
And I must thank
you for that –
the gift of
a brand new
perspective.

I used to be weary of
nights like these, ones
wherein I smile for no
reason – thinking, "when
will this end?" I was
never present. I never
allowed myself to feel.

Tonight, I'm bathing
in happiness, and life
has never felt so right.

Mindsets change like seasons.
And just like there are glimpses of
spring in winter, there are glimpses
of happiness in sadness. You just
have to be strong long enough
to make it through the cold.

Take every second from
every moment you have
ever lived and place them
in a pile out in front of you.

This stack, this benevolent,
golden architecture that rests
in front of you, it does not add
up to a lifetime, not just yet.

You are not over. You are
nowhere near the end. You
are somewhere in the middle.
You still have time to make
this life what it could be,
what you want it to be.

You were
important for
unexpected reasons:
to teach me that
holding on isn't
always the right
choice.

I held on so tightly,
I broke bones in my fingers,
hurting myself more than
you ever hurt me.

I was waiting for something
that was never going to happen,
forever stuck hanging in suspense.

Old feelings don't always return,
and sometimes, when they do, they
just stop by to say hello before
going back to where they belong.

And I couldn't live like that, knowing
that the love of my life could stop by
at any moment just to haunt me
all over again.

This realization set me free.

I've been so busy
trying to forget you,
I've forgotten the beauty
of remembering you.

It wasn't a missed connection:
it was a constant failure to connect.
And even though we tried, so damn hard,
to make the pieces fit, there's just too big
of a difference between holding hands
and holding souls.

Don't' forget:
somewhere between
hello and goodbye,
there was love,
so much love.

For the very first time
in a very long time, I woke
up today and finally felt
okay with being awake.

I did not close my eyes and
beg my mind and body and
soul for twenty more minutes.

I did not open my eyes
and feel this sudden rush of
disappointment that my reality
did not match up with what
I dreamt of last night.

I opened my eyes, smiled,
and felt this euphoric feeling,
this overwhelming sense that
I am happy to be alive, just
happy to know that I've been
gifted one more chance
to make things right.

   *- I left a window open last night,
   and joy found its way to me*

I have scars
on my fingertips
from all those nights
of crawling my way
out of unrequited
love.

My scars are
gentle reminders
that not all lovers
are gentle.

And the only regret
I have is that I ever allowed
the absence of a love from
someone else to baptize me
in a sea of self-doubt.

Untangling your fingers from mine
has been the hardest fight of my life,
because it can feel nearly impossible
to let go of something you once
planned on holding onto forever.

Sometimes,
life takes the thing
you love and places
it in front of you and
lights it on fire.

And the only way
to save yourself from
watching the thing you
adore burn is to simply
adore nothing.

This is why love
has always been so
terrifying to me; it gives
me something I may
have to watch
burn someday.

So instead,
you take numbness,
and you marry it – let
it sleep in bed with you,
carry it on your back
everywhere you go.

It is terrible, but it is safe,
and it was a choice I made
after the first few times I
watched the things I loved
become ashes on the ground.

- until I was ready again

If I wrote down on a
blank piece of paper how
I felt about the way we ended,
and if I did it day after day,
year after year after year,
I'd never run out of ink.
I'd never run out of paper.
I'd never write a single word.
I feel nothing about it now:
this is the closure I have
always truly wanted.

If you ever feel like
coming back, just don't:
I don't give second chances
to people who have
second guessed me.

*- I'm enough, and I
know this now*

I have
every reason to
never trust again,
but I refuse to miss
out on the beauty of
choosing to be
vulnerable.

If only you understood
the importance of pain;
you wouldn't be so afraid
of starting over.

- you can still be happy

Now that I'm healed,
I can look back and see this:
I think losing you hurt so much
because you gave me something
that I'd never had before, a
fighting chance at happiness.

In watching you love me, I learned how
to love myself, how to search for beauty
marks in the scars that haunt me deep
into the dead of night. So no, it wasn't
a waste of time. And no, I don't regret
a single moment spent with you.

I'm proud to say
that I survived losing you,
something I thought I never
could do. And now that I've
healed and some time has
been put behind me, I think
my heart is ready to try again.

I'm ready to stumble, fall,
fail miserably, risk getting hurt,
take a chance on someone and
something new, because, at the
end of it all, nobody gets rewarded
for a long and boring life.

Nobody talks or cares about
the person who lived long and
did nothing, the one who never
put themselves out there after
getting hurt.

I want something more.
And today, I'm choosing to retake
my very first steps toward all
I am meant for in this life.

I'm choosing to come out on the
other side of losing you a better and
happier person because we happened.

- I survived

Dear reader,

Thank you for taking the time to read this book.
I hope you allot some space within yourself for
these words of mine. I hope the most hopeful
and glimmering of them all make their way into
your bloodstream and find a home within you. I
hope you stay curious, open, inspired, hopeful,
optimistic, powerful, blissful, and every other positive
adjective there is. I hope that your lessons in life
all tally up to making you a better and happier
person. If you're reading this, you still have so
much life left to live. You have so much more
you are meant to do in this world, whether you
can see that now or not. And I know, it's hard
to see this from the low points in life. It's as if
the walls of the valley you've lost yourself in
block all light and sight of your purpose here.
The good thing is, whether you see it or not,
your purpose still exists. And if you're having
a hard time believing that, well, you'll just
have to take my word for it.

With love,
Faraway
(@farawaypoetry)

18512529R00051

Printed in Great Britain
by Amazon